naby Goes Wild

Gary Richmond

WORD PUBLISHING

Dallas · London · Vancouver · Melbourne

VIEW FROM THE ZOO STORIES are based on the real-life adventures of Gary Richmond, a veteran of the Los Angeles Zoo, minister, counselor, and camp nature speaker. Gary has three children and lives in Chino Hills, California, with his wife, Carol.

Barnaby goes wild

Copyright © 1991 by Gary Richmond for the text. Copyright © 1991 by Bruce Day for the illustrations.

Library of Congress Cataloging-in-Publication Data

Richmond, Gary, 1944-
  Barnaby goes wild/Gary Richmond; illustrated by
    Bruce Day.
    p. cm.–(A View from the zoo stories)
    Summary: A Christian zookeeper relates an anecdote
  about a baboon who escapes from the zoo but is
  happier when recaptured and returned to his cage, a
  reminder that God's church is a safe place and better
  than the world outside the church.
    ISBN 0-8499-0914-7 :
    1. Church–Juvenile literature. [1. Christian life.
  2. Baboons. 3. Zoos.] I. Day, Bruce, ill. II. Title. III.
  Series: Richmond, Gary. View from the zoo stories.
  BV600.2.R495 1991
  248.4–dc20
                                                91-757
                                                CIP
                                                AC

Printed in the United States of America

1 2 3 4 5 6 9 LBM 9 8 7 6 5 4 3 2 1

This book is dedicated to Linda Maze, my goddaughter.

Hi, I'm Gary Richmond, and I'm a zoo keeper. As a zoo keeper, I've learned a lot about God's wonderful animals. At the same time, I've learned a lot about God.

This is the story of Barnaby, a teenage baboon. (A baboon is the largest kind of monkey.) He lived with his mother and seven other baboons in a large cage in the Griffith Park Zoo.

One day Barnaby slipped past a careless zoo keeper and escaped. We didn't worry about him. Everyone knew Barnaby would stay near his baboon family. And when he got hungry, we would just catch him and put him back in the cage. Everyone knew this but Barnaby.

Barnaby was about 3 years old. He was not quite half grown, but he was full of fun and energy. He was independent and smart. When the food trap was set, Barnaby wouldn't go near it. He knew it was a trap and stayed away. But he was soon very hungry. So, he began to climb over the zoo fence to look for food in the woods around the zoo.

Barnaby was losing weight. In fact, his ribs were showing. He stayed hungry all the time. He ate a few wild berries and leaves, but it just wasn't enough for a growing baboon. He was so hungry that he even ate grasshoppers and locusts when he could catch them. Each day his search for food took him further and further away from the zoo. But he still came back at night to sleep outside his family's cage.

One day when Barnaby was looking for food, the woods suddenly ended. He stopped and looked. Green lawns and people were everywhere. And they were eating great-looking food! Barnaby was afraid of being caught. So, he stayed at the edge of the woods for a few days, watching the people. Finally, he decided he was more hungry than afraid. And he accepted a peanut butter sandwich from a smiling little boy. Wow! Compared to grasshoppers, this was great!

Barnaby began eating food given by the happy picnickers all the time. Soon, he would walk up and take it right out of their hands. He would eat until he was completely full. Barnaby was very gentle. And since he was still young and small, no one was afraid of him. But he weighed almost 40 pounds and was growing all the time.

One evening Barnaby was too full to eat any more.
So, he started back to the zoo to see his family and to sleep
as he usually did. Without knowing it, Barnaby walked
under a tree where a female mountain lion was waiting.
She was looking for something to eat. When she saw
Barnaby, she decided to follow him.

Barnaby felt uneasy. He didn't know why, but something was wrong. He wasn't hearing enough birds singing. The other animals were nervous, and he knew it. The lioness was downwind; so, Barnaby didn't catch her scent. He didn't hear her either—she was too quiet on her soft paws.

Suddenly the lioness stepped on a twig. Snap!
Barnaby heard it and began running as fast as he could
through the trees. The mountain lion heard him run, and
she chased him with all her might. When Barnaby looked
back, she was catching up to him. He leapt into an oak
tree and began to climb. His heart pounded hard when he
saw that she could climb, too. He was 30 feet up into the
branches, and she was still closing in.

The lioness was within five feet! Barnaby dropped quickly to some lower branches and fell to the ground. She leapt, too. But she was afraid of falling through the branches to the ground. So, she grabbed a tree limb and held on for a second. Then she pulled herself back into the tree.

Barnaby ran straight to the zoo fence, panting and squealing. He climbed it faster than he had ever done before. It was a close call. That night he leaned against his family's cage, holding his mother's arm for comfort while he slept.

The next week Barnaby found two coyotes eating some meat. He was hungry; so, he yelled at them in baboon language. They didn't move. He charged toward them. Still they didn't move. Finally, Barnaby picked up rocks and threw them at the female coyote. A rock hit her right on the end of her nose, and she ran away. But the male coyote stood his ground.

At last, Barnaby picked up a tree branch with dead leaves and ran at the male coyote. He was swinging the branch and yelling loudly. That was enough for the coyote. He ran away, and Barnaby had a nice meal on the meat the coyotes had left.

Barnaby now weighed 90 pounds, and the picnickers began to be afraid of him. They reported him to the park rangers. Then the rangers called the zoo and told the keepers they had to catch Barnaby. He had been on the loose in the woods for over a year.

Dr. Wordsworth at the zoo decided to wait for Barnaby to come down to be with his family that night. Then he would shoot Barnaby with the tranquilizer gun. It would put Barnaby to sleep for a while, but it wouldn't hurt him.

Barnaby came home about seven o'clock every evening. So, on Friday evening Dr. Wordsworth carefully prepared a capture dart and loaded it in the rifle.

Then he placed grapes and bananas in a pile for Barnaby and hid in some nearby bushes.

The zoo was full of animals making their wonderful, wild sounds. The gibbons were hooting. The parrots were screeching. And the lions were roaring.

At 7:02 Barnaby climbed the fence into the zoo. He walked up to the grapes and bananas slowly. They had never been there before. He wondered why they were there now. He looked carefully in every direction but didn't see anyone. So, he walked around the food and bent over to smell it.

Boom! The blast of the rifle scared Barnaby. He ran for the zoo fence. In seconds he felt a sharp sting in his leg and stopped to pull out the dart. All he had to do was get over the outside fence. Then he would be free in the woods again.

Barnaby was already feeling very woozy. He reached for the fence, but he couldn't remember why. So, he just sat down. Several animal keepers came running toward him, but he was not afraid. The medicine was working. Then everything went black as he fell asleep.

Barnaby woke up in a large cage at the health center. He had been carefully examined. The results were clear: Barnaby was one of the finest adult male baboons living in any zoo. He was soon back with his family. And he was happier than he had ever been in the woods.

Barnaby had been very gentle in the woods. But he became very strong back in his cage. He took his father's place as head of the baboon family. And he became father of many baby baboons himself.

Barnaby's home in the zoo reminds me of God's church—a safe and happy place to be. Sometimes the world outside the church sounds exciting and fun. But the truth is, the world outside the church is just as dangerous as the woods outside of Barnaby's zoo.

In fact, the Bible says that Satan is like the lioness that chased Barnaby through the woods: "The devil (Satan) is your enemy. And he goes around like a roaring lion looking for someone to eat" (1 Peter 5:8).

Now, I don't know about you, but I want to stay where it's safe and I can be happy. I'm going to stay in God's church with my Christian family. That's where I'll be happiest just as Barnaby was happiest with his family. How about you?